Welcome

I am so glad you are here! Before we begin this new session, I want to take the time and let you know that YOU have been prayed for! It is not a coincidence you are participating in this online Bible study.

My prayer for you this session is simple: **that you will grow closer to our Lord as you dig into His Word each and every day!** As you develop the discipline of being in God's Word on a daily basis, I pray you will fall in love with Him even more as you spend time reading from the Bible.

Each day before you read the assigned Scripture(s), pray and ask God to help you understand it. Invite Him to speak to you through His Word. Then listen. **It's His job to speak to you and your job to listen and obey.**

Take time to read the verses over and over again. We are told in Proverbs to *search and you will find.*

> *"Search for it like silver, and hunt for it like hidden treasure. Then you will understand."*

We are thrilled to provide many different resources for you as you participate in our online Bible study:
- <u>Ecclesiastes</u> Study Journal (print out or purchase online)
- Reading Plan
- Weekly Blog posts (Mondays, Wednesdays, & Fridays)
- Weekly Memory Verses
- Weekly Monday Videos
- Weekly Challenges
- Online community: Facebook, Twitter, Instagram, LoveGodGreatly.com
- Hashtags: #LoveGodGreatly

All of us here at Love God Greatly can't wait to get started with you and hope to see you at the finish line. **Endure, persevere, press on – and don't give up!** Let's finish well what we are beginning today. We will be here every step of the way, *cheering you on!* **We are in this together.** Fight to rise early, to push back the stress of the day, to sit alone and spend time in God's Word! I can't wait to see what God has in store for us this session!

Journey with us as we learn to **Love God Greatly** with our lives!!!

Table of Contents

Our Community

Love God Greatly consists of a beautiful community of women who use a variety of technology platforms to keep each other accountable in God's Word.

We start with a simple Bible reading plan, but it doesn't stop there.

Some gather in homes and churches locally, while others connect online with women across the globe. Whatever the method, we lovingly lock arms and unite for this purpose…

to Love God Greatly with our lives.

In today's fast-paced technology driven world, it would be easy to study God's Word in an isolated environment that lacks encouragement or support, but that isn't the intention here at Love God Greatly. God created us to live in community with Him and with those around us.

We need each other, and we live life better together.

Because of this, would you consider reaching out and studying with someone this session?

All of us have women in our lives who need friendship, accountability, and have the desire to dive into God's Word on a deeper level. Rest assured we'll be studying right alongside you - learning with you, cheering for you, enjoying sweet fellowship, and smiling from ear to ear as we watch God unite women together - intentionally connecting hearts and minds for His glory.

It's pretty unreal - this opportunity we have to not only grow closer to God through this study, but also to each other.

So here's the challenge: call your mom, your sister, your grandma, the girl across the street or the college friend across the country. Grab a group of girls from your church or workplace, or meet in a coffee shop with friends you have always wished you knew better. Utilize the beauty of connecting online for inspiration and accountability, and take opportunities to meet in person when you can.

Arm in arm and hand in hand,
let's do this thing… together.

We're proud of you.

We *really* want you to know that.

We're proud of you for making the commitment to be in God's Word… to be reading it each day and applying it to YOUR life - the beautiful life our Lord has given YOU.

Each session we offer a study journal that goes along with the verses we are reading. This journal is designed to help you interact with God's Word and learn to dig deeper - encouraging you to slow down to really reflect on what God is saying to you that day.

At *Love God Greatly*, we use the S.O.A.P. Bible study method. Before we begin, we'd like to take a moment to define this method and share WHY we recommend using it during your quiet time.

Why S.O.A.P. it?

It's one thing to simply read Scripture. But when you interact with it, intentionally slowing down to REALLY reflect on it, suddenly words start popping off the page. The SOAP method allows you to dig deeper into Scripture and see more than if you simply read the verses and then went on your merry way. We encourage you to take the time to S.O.A.P. through our Bible studies and see for yourself how much more you get out of your daily reading. You'll be amazed.

What does S.O.A.P. mean?

S- The S stands for Scripture. Physically write out the verses. You'll be amazed at what God will reveal to you just by taking the time to slow down and write out what you are reading!

O- The O stands for Observation. What do you see in the verses that you're reading? Who is the intended audience? Is there a repetition of words? What words stand out to you?

A- The A stands for Application. This is when God's Word becomes personal. What is God saying to me today? How can I apply what I just read to my own personal life? What changes do I need to make? Is there action that I need to take?

P- And finally, P stands for Prayer. Pray God's Word back to Him. Spend time thanking Him. If He has revealed something to you during this time in His Word, pray about it. If He has revealed some sin that is in your life, confess. And remember, He loves you dearly.

EXAMPLE: Read: Colossians 1:5-8

S- The faith and love that spring from the hope that is stored up for you in heaven and that you have already heard about in the word of truth, the gospel that has come to you. All over the world this gospel is bearing fruit and growing, just as it has been doing among you since the day you heard it and understood God's grace in all its truth. You learned it from Epaphras, our dear fellow servant, who is a faithful minister of Christ on our behalf, and who also told us of your love in the Spirit.

O-
- When you combine faith and love, you get hope.
- We have to remember that our hope is in heaven… it is yet to come.
- The gospel is the Word of Truth.
- The gospel is continually bearing fruit and growing from the first day to the last.
- It just takes one person to change a whole community… Epaphras.

A- God used one man, Epaphras, to change a whole town! I was reminded that we are simply called to tell others about Christ -it's God's job to spread the gospel, to grow it, and have it bear fruit. I felt today's verses were almost directly spoken to LGG… *"all over the world this gospel is bearing fruit and growing, just as it has been doing among you since the day you heard it and understood God's grace in all its truth."* It's so fun when God's Word becomes so alive and encourages us in our current situation! My passionate desire is that all the women involved in this Bible study will understand God's grace and have a thirst for His Word. Moved by this quote from my Bible commentary: ***"God's Word is not just for our information, it is for our transformation."***

P- Dear Lord, please help me to be an "Epaphras" - to tell others about You and then leave the results in Your loving hands. Please help me to understand and apply what I have read today to my life personally, thereby becoming more and more like You each and every day. Help me to live a life that bears the fruit of faith and love… anchoring my hope in heaven, not here on earth. Help me to remember that the BEST is yet to come!

———————————

Remember, the most important ingredients in the S.O.A.P. method are YOUR interaction with God's Word and your APPLICATION of His Word to YOUR life.

Blessed is the man whose *"delight is in the law of the Lord, and on his law he meditates day and night. He is like a tree planted by streams of water, which yields its fruit in season and whose leaf does not wither. Whatever he does prospers."* **~ Psalm 1:2-3**

Soap Reading Plan

		Read	SOAP
WEEK 1	Monday	Ecclesiastes 1:1-6	Ecclesiastes 1:1-2
	Tuesday	Ecclesiastes 1:7-11	Ecclesiastes 1:9-10
	Wednesday	Ecclesiastes 1:12-18	Ecclesiastes 1:17-18
	Thursday	Ecclesiastes 2:1-8	Ecclesiastes 2:1-2
	Friday	Ecclesiastes 2:9-11	Ecclesiastes 2:11
	Response Day		
WEEK 2	Monday	Ecclesiastes 2:12-17	Ecclesiastes 2:12-13
	Tuesday	Ecclesiastes 2:18-19	Ecclesiastes 2:18-19
	Wednesday	Ecclesiastes 2:20-23	Ecclesiastes 2:20-21
	Thursday	Ecclesiastes 2:24-26	Ecclesiastes 2:24-25
	Friday	Ecclesiastes 3:1-8	Ecclesiastes 3:1
	Response Day		
WEEK 3	Monday	Ecclesiastes 3:9-15	Ecclesiastes 3:14-15
	Tuesday	Ecclesiastes 3:16-22	Ecclesiastes 3:16-17
	Wednesday	Ecclesiastes 4:1-6	Ecclesiastes 4:6
	Thursday	Ecclesiastes 4:7-12	Ecclesiastes 4:9-10
	Friday	Ecclesiastes 4:13-16	Ecclesiastes 4:13
	Response Day		
WEEK 4	Monday	Ecclesiastes 5:1-7	Ecclesiastes 5:4-5
	Tuesday	Ecclesiastes 5:8-17	Ecclesiastes 5:10-12
	Wednesday	Ecclesiastes 5:18-20	Ecclesiastes 5:19
	Thursday	Ecclesiastes 6:1-6	Ecclesiastes 6:1-2
	Friday	Ecclesiastes 6:7-12	Ecclesiastes 6:10-11
	Response Day		
WEEK 5	Monday	Ecclesiastes 7:1-6	Ecclesiastes 7:1
	Tuesday	Ecclesiastes 7:7-13	Ecclesiastes 7:11-12
	Wednesday	Ecclesiastes 7:14-18	Ecclesiastes 7:14
	Thursday	Ecclesiastes 7:19-24	Ecclesiastes 7:19-20
	Friday	Ecclesiastes 7:25-29	Ecclesiastes 7:27-29
	Response Day		
WEEK 6	Monday	Ecclesiastes 8:1-9	Ecclesiastes 8:4-5
	Tuesday	Ecclesiastes 8:10-13	Ecclesiastes 8:12
	Wednesday	Ecclesiastes 8:14-15	Ecclesiastes 8:15
	Thursday	Ecclesiastes 8:16-17	Ecclesiastes 8:16-17
	Friday	Ecclesiastes 9:1-6	Ecclesiastes 9:1
	Response Day		
WEEK 7	Monday	Ecclesiastes 9:7-10	Ecclesiastes 9:10
	Tuesday	Ecclesiastes 9:11-18	Ecclesiastes 9:17-18
	Wednesday	Ecclesiastes 10:1-7	Ecclesiastes 10:1-2
	Thursday	Ecclesiastes 10:8-15	Ecclesiastes 10:12-13
	Friday	Ecclesiastes 10:16-20	Ecclesiastes 10:18
	Response Day		
WEEK 8	Monday	Ecclesiastes 11:1-4	Ecclesiastes 11:4
	Tuesday	Ecclesiastes 11:5-10	Ecclesiastes 11:8
	Wednesday	Ecclesiastes 12:1-8	Ecclesiastes 12:1-2
	Thursday	Ecclesiastes 12:9-12	Ecclesiastes 12:11
	Friday	Ecclesiastes 12:13-14	Ecclesiastes 12:13-14
	Response Day		

Goals

We believe it's important to write out goals for each session. Take some time now and write three goals you would like to focus on this session as we begin to rise each day and dig into God's Word. Make sure and refer back to these goals throughout the next eight weeks to help you stay focused. YOU CAN DO IT!!!

My goals for this session are:

1.

2.

3.

Signature: _____

Date: _____

Introduction to Ecclesiastes

It seems as though many Christians today spend a lot more time reading the New Testament than the Old Testament. But only reading one half of the Bible is sort of like only eating from one food group. Nothing but meat will lead to some trouble. Nothing but grains will deny your body of the nutrients it needs. We need to read the Old Testament. Why? The answer is found in Romans 15:4

> *For whatever was written in former days was written for our instruction, that through endurance and through the encouragement of the Scriptures we might have hope.*

This of course is true of the book of Ecclesiastes, where we find ourselves during this study.

"Vanity of Vanities… all is vanity." (Eccl. 1:2) So begins and ends one of the most difficult and challenging books of the Bible. At first glance, this book can seem like a very depressing read. It emphasizes the emptiness of life and the vanity of so many good things we experience in the world. But a careful reading will show you that the full message is God-exalting and joy-inducing.

The author of Ecclesiastes is believed by many to have been King Solomon, the son of David. Though there has been much debate in the last two centuries that perhaps it was written by someone who lived after Solomon and whose name we do not know.

Either way, Ecclesiastes evaluates life lived with God and apart from Him.

You will notice that Solomon tends to jump from topic to topic. Some of the themes that he explores are the following:
- This world is corrupt, temporal, confusing, and seemingly unfair.
- We are not God and therefore do not always understand what He is doing.
- Wisdom is better than folly.
- Worldly things do not last and are of little value.
- Death comes to everyone.
- True satisfaction cannot be found in earthly things.

The main idea of the book of Ecclesiastes is that life is meaningless unless a person knows God. For life without God is little more than a series of experiences that leads every person, whether rich or poor, moral or immoral, to the grave. A sharp mind is great but it fades with age, and even wisdom grows dull. Wealth seems so desirable and helpful, but it can be taken from us through unfortunate events. Even if we hold on to it, it can't go with us past the grave.

Solomon's conclusion is that in order for one to find meaning, purpose, and satisfaction in life he or she must know God. To know the Lord, loving Him, fearing Him, following Him, and finding our identity in Him is what frees us to enjoy the temporal gifts in this life and to look beyond those gifts to life everlasting.

"Let all that is empty here on Earth, lead you to what alone will satisfy — the grace of God, the love of God, the Lamb of God; to "Jesus Christ, the same yesterday, today, and forever." (Hebrews 13:8)

- George Mylne, (1859)

Looking to Jesus,

Jen

Week 1

Week 1 Challenge (Note: You can find this listed in our Monday blog post):

Prayer focus for this week: Spend time praying for your family members.

	Praying	Praise
Monday		
Tuesday		
Wednesday		
Thursday		
Friday		

What has been is what will be, and what has been done is what will be done, and there is nothing new under the sun.

Ecclesiastes 1:9 (ESV)

Scripture for Week 1

MONDAY

ECCLESIASTES 1:1-6 (ESV)

[1] The words of the Preacher, the son of David, king in Jerusalem. [2] Vanity of vanities, says the Preacher, vanity of vanities! All is vanity.[3] What does man gain by all the toil at which he toils under the sun? [4] A generation goes, and a generation comes, but the earth remains forever. [5] The sun rises, and the sun goes down, and hastens to the place where it rises. [6] The wind blows to the south and goes around to the north; around and around goes the wind, and on its circuits the wind returns.

TUESDAY

ECCLESIASTES 1:7-11 (ESV)

[7] All streams run to the sea, but the sea is not full; to the place where the streams flow, there they flow again. [8] All things are full of weariness; a man cannot utter it; the eye is not satisfied with seeing, nor the ear filled with hearing. [9] What has been is what will be, and what has been done is what will be done, and there is nothing new under the sun. [10] Is there a thing of which it is said, "See, this is new"? It has been already in the ages before us. [11] There is no remembrance of former things, nor will there be any remembrance of later things yet to be among those who come after.

WEDNESDAY

ECCLESIASTES 1:12-18 (ESV)

[12] I the Preacher have been king over Israel in Jerusalem. [13] And I applied my heart to seek and to search out by wisdom all that is done under heaven. It is an unhappy business that God has given to the children of man to be busy with. [14] I have seen everything that is done under the sun, and behold, all is vanity and a striving after wind.

[15] What is crooked cannot be made straight, and what is lacking cannot be counted.

[16] I said in my heart, "I have acquired great wisdom, surpassing all who were over Jerusalem before me, and my heart has had great experience of wisdom and knowledge." [17] And I applied my heart to know wisdom and to know madness and folly. I perceived that this also is but a striving after wind.

[18] For in much wisdom is much vexation, and he who increases knowledge increases sorrow.

THURSDAY   *ECCLESIASTES 2:1-8 (ESV)*

[1] I said in my heart, "Come now, I will test you with pleasure; enjoy yourself." But behold, this also was vanity. [2] I said of laughter, "It is mad," and of pleasure, "What use is it?" [3] I searched with my heart how to cheer my body with wine—my heart still guiding me with wisdom—and how to lay hold on folly, till I might see what was good for the children of man to do under heaven during the few days of their life. [4] I made great works. I built houses and planted vineyards for myself. [5] I made myself gardens and parks, and planted in them all kinds of fruit trees. [6] I made myself pools from which to water the forest of growing trees. [7] I bought male and female slaves, and had slaves who were born in my house. I had also great possessions of herds and flocks, more than any who had been before me in Jerusalem. [8] I also gathered for myself silver and gold and the treasure of kings and provinces. I got singers, both men and women, and many concubines, the delight of the sons of man.

FRIDAY   *ECCLESIASTES 2:9-11 (ESV)*

[9] So I became great and surpassed all who were before me in Jerusalem. Also my wisdom remained with me. [10] And whatever my eyes desired I did not keep from them. I kept my heart from no pleasure, for my heart found pleasure in all my toil, and this was my reward for all my toil. [11] Then I considered all that my hands had done and the toil I had expended in doing it, and behold, all was vanity and a striving after wind, and there was nothing to be gained under the sun.

Read: Ecclesiastes 1:1-6
Soap: Ecclesiastes 1:1-2

Scripture - Write out the **Scripture** passage for the day.

Observations - Write down 1 or 2 **observations** from the passage.

Applications - Write down 1 or 2 **applications** from the passage.

Pray - Write out a **prayer** over what you learned from today's passage.

Read: Ecclesiastes 1:7-11
Soap: Ecclesiastes 1:9-10

Scripture - Write out the **Scripture** passage for the day.

Observations - Write down 1 or 2 **observations** from the passage.

Tuesday

Applications - Write down 1 or 2 **applications** from the passage.

Pray - Write out a **prayer** over what you learned from today's passage.

Wednesday

Read: Ecclesiastes 1:12-18
Soap: Ecclesiastes 1:17-18

Scripture - Write out the **Scripture** passage for the day.

Observations - Write down 1 or 2 **observations** from the passage.

Wednesday

Applications - Write down 1 or 2 **applications** from the passage.

Pray - Write out a **prayer** over what you learned from today's passage.

Read: Ecclesiastes 2:1-8
Soap: Ecclesiastes 2:1-2

Scripture - Write out the **Scripture** passage for the day.

Observations - Write down 1 or 2 **observations** from the passage.

Applications - Write down 1 or 2 **applications** from the passage.

Pray - Write out a **prayer** over what you learned from today's passage.

Read: Ecclesiastes 2:9-11
Soap: Ecclesiastes 2:11

Scripture - Write out the **Scripture** passage for the day.

Observations - Write down 1 or 2 **observations** from the passage.

Applications - Write down 1 or 2 **applications** from the passage.

Pray - Write out a **prayer** over what you learned from today's passage.

Reflection Questions

1. What sweeping statement does Solomon make about life?

2. What does Solomon devote himself to?

3. Read Eccl. 1:17 and compare it to Proverbs 4:7.

4. List all the things for which Solomon indulged in Eccl. 2:1-11.

5. What do you try to find your value in?

My Response

Week 2

Week 2 Challenge (Note: You can find this listed in our Monday blog post):

Prayer focus for this week: Spend time praying for your country.

	Praying	Praise
Monday		
Tuesday		
Wednesday		
Thursday		
Friday		

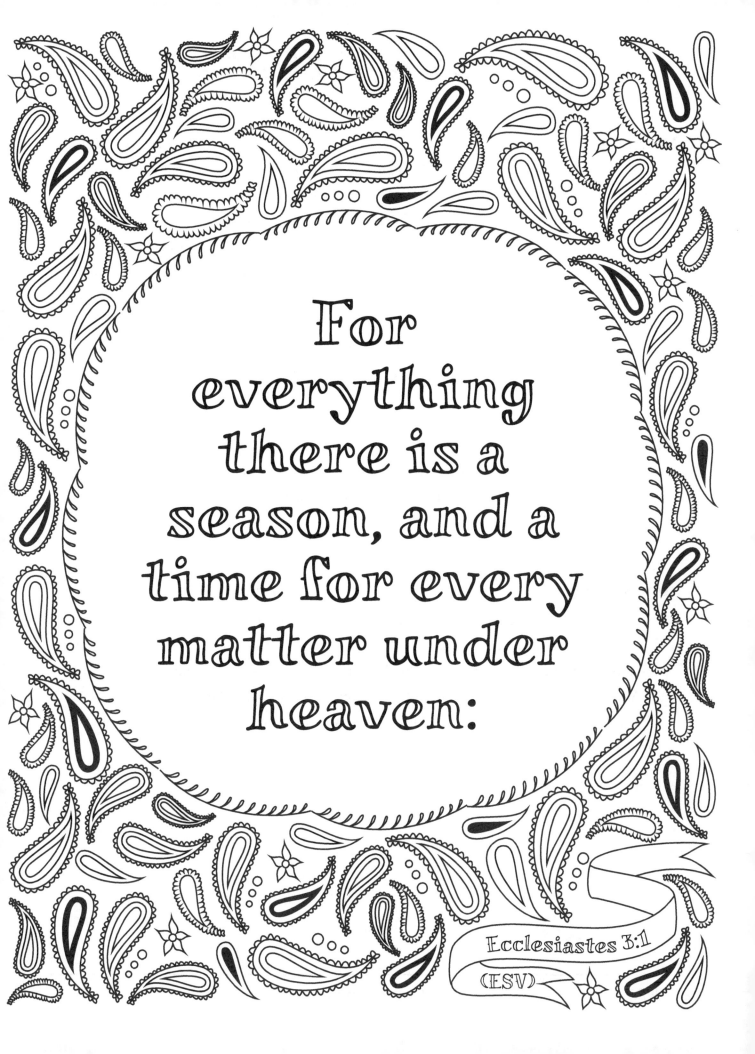

For everything there is a season, and a time for every matter under heaven:

Ecclesiastes 3:1 (ESV)

Scripture for Week 2

MONDAY *ECCLESIASTES 2:12-17 (ESV)*

¹² So I turned to consider wisdom and madness and folly. For what can the man do who comes after the king? Only what has already been done. ¹³ Then I saw that there is more gain in wisdom than in folly, as there is more gain in light than in darkness. ¹⁴ The wise person has his eyes in his head, but the fool walks in darkness. And yet I perceived that the same event happens to all of them. ¹⁵ Then I said in my heart, "What happens to the fool will happen to me also. Why then have I been so very wise?" And I said in my heart that this also is vanity. ¹⁶ For of the wise as of the fool there is no enduring remembrance, seeing that in the days to come all will have been long forgotten. How the wise dies just like the fool! ¹⁷ So I hated life, because what is done under the sun was grievous to me, for all is vanity and a striving after wind.

TUESDAY *ECCLESIASTES 2:18-19 (ESV)*

¹⁸ I hated all my toil in which I toil under the sun, seeing that I must leave it to the man who will come after me, ¹⁹ and who knows whether he will be wise or a fool? Yet he will be master of all for which I toiled and used my wisdom under the sun. This also is vanity.

WEDNESDAY *ECCLESIASTES 2:20-23 (ESV)*

²⁰ So I turned about and gave my heart up to despair over all the toil of my labors under the sun, ²¹ because sometimes a person who has toiled with wisdom and knowledge and skill must leave everything to be enjoyed by someone who did not toil for it. This also is vanity and a great evil. ²² What has a man from all the toil and striving of heart with which he toils beneath the sun? ²³ For all his days are full of sorrow, and his work is a vexation. Even in the night his heart does not rest. This also is vanity.

THURSDAY

[24] There is nothing better for a person than that he should eat and drink and find enjoyment in his toil. This also, I saw, is from the hand of God, [25] for apart from him who can eat or who can have enjoyment? [26] For to the one who pleases him God has given wisdom and knowledge and joy, but to the sinner he has given the business of gathering and collecting, only to give to one who pleases God. This also is vanity and a striving after wind.

FRIDAY

[1] For everything there is a season, and a time for every matter under heaven:

[2] a time to be born, and a time to die;

a time to plant, and a time to pluck up what is planted;

[3] a time to kill, and a time to heal;

a time to break down, and a time to build up;

[4] a time to weep, and a time to laugh;

a time to mourn, and a time to dance;

[5] a time to cast away stones, and a time to gather stones together;

a time to embrace, and a time to refrain from embracing;

[6] a time to seek, and a time to lose;

a time to keep, and a time to cast away;

[7] a time to tear, and a time to sew;

a time to keep silence, and a time to speak;

[8] a time to love, and a time to hate;

a time for war, and a time for peace.

Read: Ecclesiastes 2:12-17
Soap: Ecclesiastes 2:12-13

Scripture - Write out the **Scripture** passage for the day.

Observations - Write down 1 or 2 **observations** from the passage.

Applications - Write down 1 or 2 **applications** from the passage.

Pray - Write out a **prayer** over what you learned from today's passage.

Read: Ecclesiastes 2:18-19
Soap: Ecclesiastes 2:18-19

Scripture - Write out the **Scripture** passage for the day.

Observations - Write down 1 or 2 **observations** from the passage.

Applications - Write down 1 or 2 **applications** from the passage.

Pray - Write out a **prayer** over what you learned from today's passage.

Read: Ecclesiastes 2: 20-23
Soap: Ecclesiastes 2:20-21

Scripture - Write out the **Scripture** passage for the day.

Observations - Write down 1 or 2 **observations** from the passage.

Wednesday

Applications - Write down 1 or 2 **applications** from the passage.

Pray - Write out a **prayer** over what you learned from today's passage.

Read: Ecclesiastes 2:24-26
Soap: Ecclesiastes 2:24-25

Scripture - Write out the **Scripture** passage for the day.

Observations - Write down 1 or 2 **observations** from the passage.

Applications - Write down 1 or 2 **applications** from the passage.

Pray - Write out a **prayer** over what you learned from today's passage.

Friday

Read: Ecclesiastes 3:1-8
Soap: Ecclesiastes 3:1

Scripture - Write out the **Scripture** passage for the day.

Observations - Write down 1 or 2 **observations** from the passage.

Friday

Applications - Write down 1 or 2 **applications** from the passage.

Pray - Write out a **prayer** over what you learned from today's passage.

Reflection Questions

1. What conclusion does Solomon make regarding wisdom and folly? (Eccl. 2:16)

2. Why do you think this made him hate life? (Eccl. 2:17)

3. What is the value of work?

4. Eccl. 3:1-8 is a well-known passage. What does it teach about God and about man?

5. How should the above passage affect our everyday life?

My Response

Week 3 Challenge (Note: You can find this listed in our Monday blog post):

Prayer focus for this week: Spend time praying for your friends.

	Praying	*Praise*
Monday		
Tuesday		
Wednesday		
Thursday		
Friday		

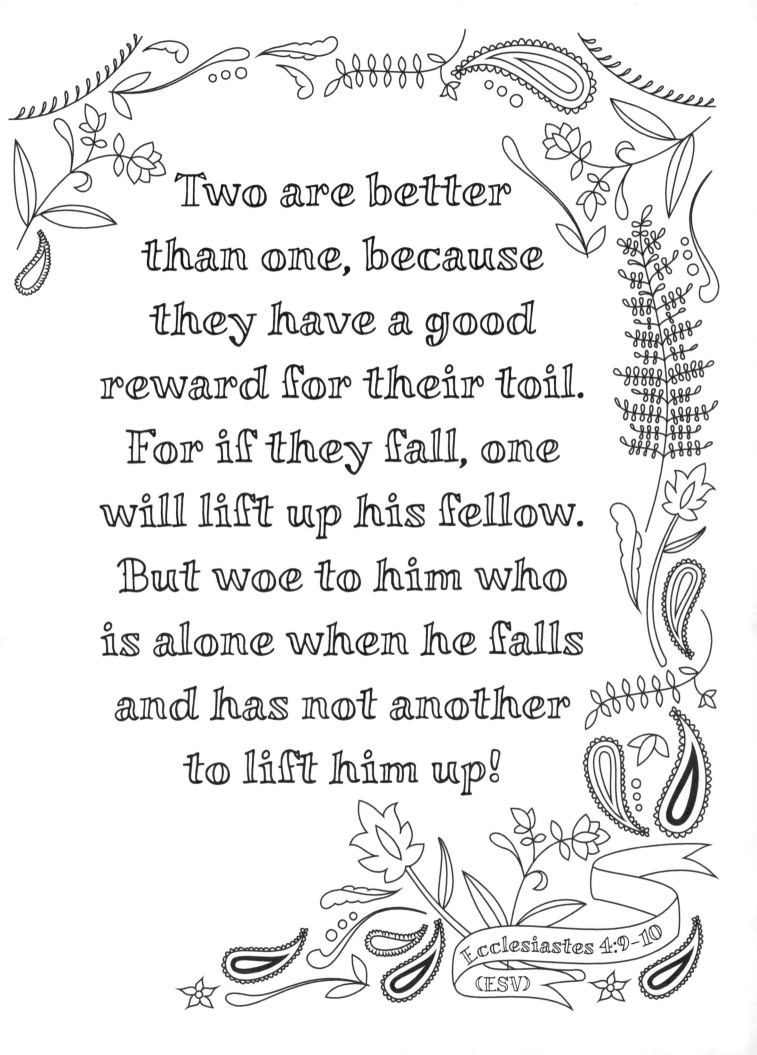

Two are better than one, because they have a good reward for their toil. For if they fall, one will lift up his fellow. But woe to him who is alone when he falls and has not another to lift him up!

Ecclesiastes 4:9-10
(ESV)

MONDAY   *ECCLESIASTES 3:9-15 (ESV)*

[9] What gain has the worker from his toil? [10] I have seen the business that God has given to the children of man to be busy with. [11] He has made everything beautiful in its time. Also, he has put eternity into man's heart, yet so that he cannot find out what God has done from the beginning to the end. [12] I perceived that there is nothing better for them than to be joyful and to do good as long as they live; [13] also that everyone should eat and drink and take pleasure in all his toil—this is God's gift to man.

[14] I perceived that whatever God does endures forever; nothing can be added to it, nor anything taken from it. God has done it, so that people fear before him. [15] That which is, already has been; that which is to be, already has been; and God seeks what has been driven away.

TUESDAY   *ECCLESIASTES 3:16-22 (ESV)*

[16] Moreover, I saw under the sun that in the place of justice, even there was wickedness, and in the place of righteousness, even there was wickedness. [17] I said in my heart, God will judge the righteous and the wicked, for there is a time for every matter and for every work. [18] I said in my heart with regard to the children of man that God is testing them that they may see that they themselves are but beasts. [19] For what happens to the children of man and what happens to the beasts is the same; as one dies, so dies the other. They all have the same breath, and man has no advantage over the beasts, for all is vanity. [20] All go to one place. All are from the dust, and to dust all return. [21] Who knows whether the spirit of man goes upward and the spirit of the beast goes down into the earth? [22] So I saw that there is nothing better than that a man should rejoice in his work, for that is his lot. Who can bring him to see what will be after him?

WEDNESDAY

[1] Again I saw all the oppressions that are done under the sun. And behold, the tears of the oppressed, and they had no one to comfort them! On the side of their oppressors there was power, and there was no one to comfort them. [2] And I thought the dead who are already dead more fortunate than the living who are still alive. [3] But better than both is he who has not yet been and has not seen the evil deeds that are done under the sun. [4] Then I saw that all toil and all skill in work come from a man's envy of his neighbor. This also is vanity and a striving after wind. [5] The fool folds his hands and eats his own flesh. [6] Better is a handful of quietness than two hands full of toil and a striving after wind.

THURSDAY

[7] Again, I saw vanity under the sun: [8] one person who has no other, either son or brother, yet there is no end to all his toil, and his eyes are never satisfied with riches, so that he never asks, "For whom am I toiling and depriving myself of pleasure?" This also is vanity and an unhappy business. [9] Two are better than one, because they have a good reward for their toil. [10] For if they fall, one will lift up his fellow. But woe to him who is alone when he falls and has not another to lift him up! [11] Again, if two lie together, they keep warm, but how can one keep warm alone? [12] And though a man might prevail against one who is alone, two will withstand him—a threefold cord is not quickly broken.

FRIDAY

[13] Better was a poor and wise youth than an old and foolish king who no longer knew how to take advice. [14] For he went from prison to the throne, though in his own kingdom he had been born poor. [15] I saw all the living who move about under the sun, along with that youth who was to stand in the king's place. [16] There was no end of all the people, all of whom he led. Yet those who come later will not rejoice in him. Surely this also is vanity and a striving after wind.

Read: Ecclesiastes 3:9-15
Soap: Ecclesiastes 3:14-15

Scripture - Write out the **Scripture** passage for the day.

Observations - Write down 1 or 2 **observations** from the passage.

Monday

Applications - Write down 1 or 2 **applications** from the passage.

Pray - Write out a **prayer** over what you learned from today's passage.

Tuesday

Read: Ecclesiastes 3:16-22
Soap: Ecclesiastes 3:16-17

Scripture - Write out the **Scripture** passage for the day.

Observations - Write down 1 or 2 **observations** from the passage.

Applications - Write down 1 or 2 **applications** from the passage.

Pray - Write out a **prayer** over what you learned from today's passage.

Read: Ecclesiastes 4:1-6
Soap: Ecclesiastes 4:6

Scripture - Write out the **Scripture** passage for the day.

Observations - Write down 1 or 2 **observations** from the passage.

Wednesday

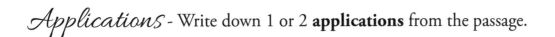

Applications - Write down 1 or 2 **applications** from the passage.

Pray - Write out a **prayer** over what you learned from today's passage.

Read: Ecclesiastes 4:7-12
Soap: Ecclesiastes 4:9-10

Scripture - Write out the **Scripture** passage for the day.

Observations - Write down 1 or 2 **observations** from the passage.

Applications - Write down 1 or 2 **applications** from the passage.

Pray - Write out a **prayer** over what you learned from today's passage.

Friday

Read: Ecclesiastes 4:13-16
Soap: Ecclesiastes 4:13

Scripture - Write out the **Scripture** passage for the day.

Observations - Write down 1 or 2 **observations** from the passage.

Applications - Write down 1 or 2 **applications** from the passage.

Pray - Write out a **prayer** over what you learned from today's passage.

Reflection Questions

1. What gift did God give to man according to Eccl. 3:13?

2. According to Eccl. 3:18 why does God test man?

3. Why does Solomon compare man to animals? (Eccl. 3:19-21)

4. What is the theme of Eccl. chapter 4?

5. In Eccl. 4:9 we are told that two are better than one. What does this mean, and what is the purpose of friendship?

My Response

Week 4 Challenge (Note: You can find this listed in our Monday blog post):

Prayer focus for this week: Spend time praying for your church.

	Praying	Praise
Monday		
Tuesday		
Wednesday		
Thursday		
Friday		

As he came from his mother's womb he shall go again, naked as he came, and shall take nothing for his toil that he may carry away in his hand.

Ecclesiastes 5:15 (ESV)

Scripture for Week 4

MONDAY   *ECCLESIASTES 5:1-7 (ESV)*

[1] Guard your steps when you go to the house of God. To draw near to listen is better than to offer the sacrifice of fools, for they do not know that they are doing evil. [2] Be not rash with your mouth, nor let your heart be hasty to utter a word before God, for God is in heaven and you are on earth. Therefore let your words be few. [3] For a dream comes with much business, and a fool's voice with many words. [4] When you vow a vow to God, do not delay paying it, for he has no pleasure in fools. Pay what you vow. [5] It is better that you should not vow than that you should vow and not pay. [6] Let not your mouth lead you into sin, and do not say before the messenger that it was a mistake. Why should God be angry at your voice and destroy the work of your hands? [7] For when dreams increase and words grow many, there is vanity; but God is the one you must fear.

TUESDAY   *ECCLESIASTES 5:8-17 (ESV)*

[8] If you see in a province the oppression of the poor and the violation of justice and righteousness, do not be amazed at the matter, for the high official is watched by a higher, and there are yet higher ones over them. [9] But this is gain for a land in every way: a king committed to cultivated fields.

[10] He who loves money will not be satisfied with money, nor he who loves wealth with his income; this also is vanity. [11] When goods increase, they increase who eat them, and what advantage has their owner but to see them with his eyes? [12] Sweet is the sleep of a laborer, whether he eats little or much, but the full stomach of the rich will not let him sleep.

[13] There is a grievous evil that I have seen under the sun: riches were kept by their owner to his hurt, [14] and those riches were lost in a bad venture. And he is father of a son, but he has nothing in his hand. [15] As he came from his mother's womb he shall go again, naked as he came, and shall take nothing for his toil that he may carry away in his hand. [16] This also is a grievous evil: just as he came, so shall he go, and what gain is there to him who toils for the wind? [17] Moreover, all his days he eats in darkness in much vexation and sickness and anger.

WEDNESDAY

ECCLESIASTES 5:18-20 (ESV)

[18] Behold, what I have seen to be good and fitting is to eat and drink and find enjoyment in all the toil with which one toils under the sun the few days of his life that God has given him, for this is his lot. [19] Everyone also to whom God has given wealth and possessions and power to enjoy them, and to accept his lot and rejoice in his toil—this is the gift of God. [20] For he will not much remember the days of his life because God keeps him occupied with joy in his heart.

THURSDAY

ECCLESIASTES 6:1-6 (ESV)

[1] There is an evil that I have seen under the sun, and it lies heavy on mankind: [2] a man to whom God gives wealth, possessions, and honor, so that he lacks nothing of all that he desires, yet God does not give him power to enjoy them, but a stranger enjoys them. This is vanity; it is a grievous evil. [3] If a man fathers a hundred children and lives many years, so that the days of his years are many, but his soul is not satisfied with life's good things, and he also has no burial, I say that a stillborn child is better off than he. [4] For it comes in vanity and goes in darkness, and in darkness its name is covered. [5] Moreover, it has not seen the sun or known anything, yet it finds rest rather than he. [6] Even though he should live a thousand years twice over, yet enjoy no good—do not all go to the one place?

FRIDAY

ECCLESIASTES 6:7-12 (ESV)

[7] All the toil of man is for his mouth, yet his appetite is not satisfied. [8] For what advantage has the wise man over the fool? And what does the poor man have who knows how to conduct himself before the living? [9] Better is the sight of the eyes than the wandering of the appetite: this also is vanity and a striving after wind.

[10] Whatever has come to be has already been named, and it is known what man is, and that he is not able to dispute with one stronger than he. [11] The more words, the more vanity, and what is the advantage to man? [12] For who knows what is good for man while he lives the few days of his vain life, which he passes like a shadow? For who can tell man what will be after him under the sun?

Monday

Read: Ecclesiastes 5:1-7
Soap: Ecclesiastes 5:4-5

Scripture - Write out the **Scripture** passage for the day.

Observations - Write down 1 or 2 **observations** from the passage.

Applications - Write down 1 or 2 **applications** from the passage.

Pray - Write out a **prayer** over what you learned from today's passage.

Tuesday

Read: Ecclesiastes 5:8-17
Soap: Ecclesiastes 5:10-12

Scripture - Write out the **Scripture** passage for the day.

Observations - Write down 1 or 2 **observations** from the passage.

Applications - Write down 1 or 2 **applications** from the passage.

Pray - Write out a **prayer** over what you learned from today's passage.

Read: Ecclesiastes 5:18-20
Soap: Ecclesiastes 5:19

Scripture - Write out the **Scripture** passage for the day.

Observations - Write down 1 or 2 **observations** from the passage.

Applications - Write down 1 or 2 **applications** from the passage.

Pray - Write out a **prayer** over what you learned from today's passage.

Read: Ecclesiastes 6:1-6
Soap: Ecclesiastes 6:1-2

Scripture - Write out the **Scripture** passage for the day.

Observations - Write down 1 or 2 **observations** from the passage.

Thursday

Applications - Write down 1 or 2 **applications** from the passage.

Pray - Write out a **prayer** over what you learned from today's passage.

Friday

Read: Ecclesiastes 6:7-12
Soap: Ecclesiastes 6:10-11

Scripture - Write out the **Scripture** passage for the day.

Observations - Write down 1 or 2 **observations** from the passage.

Friday

Applications - Write down 1 or 2 **applications** from the passage.

Pray - Write out a **prayer** over what you learned from today's passage.

Reflection Questions

1. What are sacrifices of fools? (Eccl. 5:1)

2. What does it mean to fear the Lord? How can you grow in this area?

3. Why is it vanity to love money and wealth?

4. In Eccl. 5:18 we are told that we are to enjoy the work that God has given us. Make a list of all the tasks God regularly calls you to do. Do you find joy in them? If not, how can you become more joyful?

5. In Eccl. 6:3-4 Solomon makes a pretty shocking statement. What is the meaning of these verses?

My Response

Week 5 Challenge (Note: You can find this listed in our Monday blog post):

Prayer focus for this week: Spend time praying for missionaries.

	Praying	Praise
Monday		
Tuesday		
Wednesday		
Thursday		
Friday		

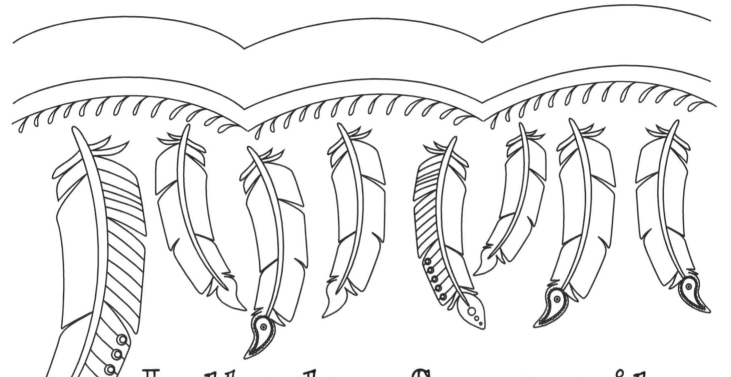

In the day of prosperity be joyful, and in the day of adversity consider: God has made the one as well as the other, so that man may not find out anything that will be after him.

Ecclesiastes 7:14 (ESV)

Scripture for Week 5

MONDAY   *ECCLESIASTES 7:1-6 (ESV)*

1 A good name is better than precious ointment,
and the day of death than the day of birth.

2 It is better to go to the house of mourning
than to go to the house of feasting,
for this is the end of all mankind,
and the living will lay it to heart.

3 Sorrow is better than laughter,
for by sadness of face the heart is made glad.

4 The heart of the wise is in the house of mourning,
but the heart of fools is in the house of mirth.

5 It is better for a man to hear the rebuke of the wise
than to hear the song of fools.

6 For as the crackling of thorns under a pot,
so is the laughter of the fools;
this also is vanity.

TUESDAY   *ECCLESIASTES 7:7-13 (ESV)*

7 Surely oppression drives the wise into madness,
and a bribe corrupts the heart.

8 Better is the end of a thing than its beginning,
and the patient in spirit is better than the proud in spirit.

9 Be not quick in your spirit to become angry,
for anger lodges in the heart of fools.

10 Say not, "Why were the former days better than these?"
For it is not from wisdom that you ask this.

11 Wisdom is good with an inheritance,
an advantage to those who see the sun.

12 For the protection of wisdom is like the protection of money,
and the advantage of knowledge is that wisdom preserves the life of him who has it.

13 Consider the work of God:
who can make straight what he has made crooked?

WEDNESDAY

ECCLESIASTES 7:14-18 (ESV)

[14] In the day of prosperity be joyful, and in the day of adversity consider: God has made the one as well as the other, so that man may not find out anything that will be after him.

[15] In my vain life I have seen everything. There is a righteous man who perishes in his righteousness, and there is a wicked man who prolongs his life in his evildoing. [16] Be not overly righteous, and do not make yourself too wise. Why should you destroy yourself? [17] Be not overly wicked, neither be a fool. Why should you die before your time? [18] It is good that you should take hold of this, and from that withhold not your hand, for the one who fears God shall come out from both of them.

THURSDAY

ECCLESIASTES 7:19-24 (ESV)

[19] Wisdom gives strength to the wise man more than ten rulers who are in a city.

[20] Surely there is not a righteous man on earth who does good and never sins.

[21] Do not take to heart all the things that people say, lest you hear your servant cursing you.

[22] Your heart knows that many times you yourself have cursed others.

[23] All this I have tested by wisdom. I said, "I will be wise," but it was far from me. [24] That which has been is far off, and deep, very deep; who can find it out?

FRIDAY

ECCLESIASTES 7:25-29 (ESV)

[25] I turned my heart to know and to search out and to seek wisdom and the scheme of things, and to know the wickedness of folly and the foolishness that is madness. [26] And I find something more bitter than death: the woman whose heart is snares and nets, and whose hands are fetters. He who pleases God escapes her, but the sinner is taken by her. [27] Behold, this is what I found, says the Preacher, while adding one thing to another to find the scheme of things— [28] which my soul has sought repeatedly, but I have not found. One man among a thousand I found, but a woman among all these I have not found. [29] See, this alone I found, that God made man upright, but they have sought out many schemes.

Monday

Read: Ecclesiastes 7:1-6
Soap: Ecclesiastes 7:1

Scripture - Write out the **Scripture** passage for the day.

Observations - Write down 1 or 2 **observations** from the passage.

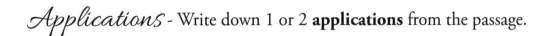

Applications - Write down 1 or 2 **applications** from the passage.

Pray - Write out a **prayer** over what you learned from today's passage.

Read: Ecclesiastes 7:7-13
Soap: Ecclesiastes 7:11-12

Scripture - Write out the **Scripture** passage for the day.

Observations - Write down 1 or 2 **observations** from the passage.

Tuesday

Applications - Write down 1 or 2 **applications** from the passage.

Pray - Write out a **prayer** over what you learned from today's passage.

Wednesday

Read: Ecclesiastes 7:14-18
Soap: Ecclesiastes 7:14

Scripture - Write out the **Scripture** passage for the day.

Observations - Write down 1 or 2 **observations** from the passage.

Wednesday

Applications - Write down 1 or 2 **applications** from the passage.

Pray - Write out a **prayer** over what you learned from today's passage.

Read: Ecclesiastes 7:19-24
Soap: Ecclesiastes 7:19-20

Scripture - Write out the **Scripture** passage for the day.

Observations - Write down 1 or 2 **observations** from the passage.

Thursday

Applications - Write down 1 or 2 **applications** from the passage.

Pray - Write out a **prayer** over what you learned from today's passage.

Read: Ecclesiastes 7:25-29
Soap: Ecclesiastes 7:27-29

Scripture - Write out the **Scripture** passage for the day.

Observations - Write down 1 or 2 **observations** from the passage.

Friday

Applications - Write down 1 or 2 **applications** from the passage.

Pray - Write out a **prayer** over what you learned from today's passage.

Reflection Questions

1. Why is "mourning" better than "feasting" and "sorrow" better than "laughter"? (Eccl. 7:1-4)

2. Make a list of what is wise and what is foolishness according to Eccl. chapter 7.

3. Why is anger dangerous according to Eccl. 7:9?

4. In Eccl. 7:16 we are told to not be overly righteous or too wise. Is this possible? What does Solomon mean?

5. After many observations Solomon comes to a conclusion in Eccl. 7:29. What is his conclusion?

My Response

Week 6

Week 6 Challenge (Note: You can find this listed in our Monday blog post):

Prayer focus for this week: Spend time praying for you.

	Praying	Praise
Monday		
Tuesday		
Wednesday		
Thursday		
Friday		

Though a sinner does evil a hundred times and prolongs his life, yet I know that it will be well with those who fear God, because they fear before him.

Ecclesiastes 8:12 (ESV)

Scripture for Week 6

MONDAY   *ECCLESIASTES 8:1-9 (ESV)*

¹ Who is like the wise?

   And who knows the interpretation of a thing?

A man's wisdom makes his face shine,

   and the hardness of his face is changed.

² I say: Keep the king's command, because of God's oath to him. ³ Be not hasty to go from his presence. Do not take your stand in an evil cause, for he does whatever he pleases. ⁴ For the word of the king is supreme, and who may say to him, "What are you doing?" ⁵ Whoever keeps a command will know no evil thing, and the wise heart will know the proper time and the just way. ⁶ For there is a time and a way for everything, although man's trouble lies heavy on him. ⁷ For he does not know what is to be, for who can tell him how it will be? ⁸ No man has power to retain the spirit, or power over the day of death. There is no discharge from war, nor will wickedness deliver those who are given to it. ⁹ All this I observed while applying my heart to all that is done under the sun, when man had power over man to his hurt.

TUESDAY   *ECCLESIASTES 8:10-13 (ESV)*

¹⁰ Then I saw the wicked buried. They used to go in and out of the holy place and were praised in the city where they had done such things. This also is vanity. ¹¹ Because the sentence against an evil deed is not executed speedily, the heart of the children of man is fully set to do evil. ¹² Though a sinner does evil a hundred times and prolongs his life, yet I know that it will be well with those who fear God, because they fear before him. ¹³ But it will not be well with the wicked, neither will he prolong his days like a shadow, because he does not fear before God.

WEDNESDAY   *ECCLESIASTES 8:14-15 (ESV)*

¹⁴ There is a vanity that takes place on earth, that there are righteous people to whom it happens according to the deeds of the wicked, and there are wicked people to whom it happens according to the deeds of the righteous. I said that this also is vanity. ¹⁵ And I commend joy, for man has nothing better under the sun but to eat and drink and be joyful, for this will go with him in his toil through the days of his life that God has given him under the sun.

THURSDAY

[16] When I applied my heart to know wisdom, and to see the business that is done on earth, how neither day nor night do one's eyes see sleep, [17] then I saw all the work of God, that man cannot find out the work that is done under the sun. However much man may toil in seeking, he will not find it out. Even though a wise man claims to know, he cannot find it out.

FRIDAY

[1] But all this I laid to heart, examining it all, how the righteous and the wise and their deeds are in the hand of God. Whether it is love or hate, man does not know; both are before him. [2] It is the same for all, since the same event happens to the righteous and the wicked, to the good and the evil, to the clean and the unclean, to him who sacrifices and him who does not sacrifice. As the good one is, so is the sinner, and he who swears is as he who shuns an oath. [3] This is an evil in all that is done under the sun, that the same event happens to all. Also, the hearts of the children of man are full of evil, and madness is in their hearts while they live, and after that they go to the dead. [4] But he who is joined with all the living has hope, for a living dog is better than a dead lion. [5] For the living know that they will die, but the dead know nothing, and they have no more reward, for the memory of them is forgotten. [6] Their love and their hate and their envy have already perished, and forever they have no more share in all that is done under the sun.

Read: Ecclesiastes 8:1-9
Soap: Ecclesiastes 8:4-5

Scripture - Write out the **Scripture** passage for the day.

Observations - Write down 1 or 2 **observations** from the passage.

Applications - Write down 1 or 2 **applications** from the passage.

Pray - Write out a **prayer** over what you learned from today's passage.

Tuesday

Read: Ecclesiastes 8:10-13
Soap: Ecclesiastes 8:12

Scripture - Write out the **Scripture** passage for the day.

Observations - Write down 1 or 2 **observations** from the passage.

Tuesday

Applications - Write down 1 or 2 **applications** from the passage.

Pray - Write out a **prayer** over what you learned from today's passage.

Wednesday

Read: Ecclesiastes 8:14-15
Soap: Ecclesiastes 8:15

Scripture - Write out the **Scripture** passage for the day.

Observations - Write down 1 or 2 **observations** from the passage.

Wednesday

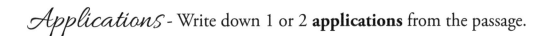

Applications - Write down 1 or 2 **applications** from the passage.

Pray - Write out a **prayer** over what you learned from today's passage.

Read: Ecclesiastes 8:16-17
Soap: Ecclesiastes 8:16-17

Scripture - Write out the **Scripture** passage for the day.

Observations - Write down 1 or 2 **observations** from the passage.

Thursday

Applications - Write down 1 or 2 **applications** from the passage.

Pray - Write out a **prayer** over what you learned from today's passage.

Read: Ecclesiastes 9:1-6
Soap: Ecclesiastes 9:1

Scripture - Write out the **Scripture** passage for the day.

Observations - Write down 1 or 2 **observations** from the passage.

Friday

Applications - Write down 1 or 2 **applications** from the passage.

Pray - Write out a **prayer** over what you learned from today's passage.

-Visit our website today for the corresponding blog post!-

Reflection Questions

1. What effect does wisdom have on a person according to Eccl. 8:1?

2. Why does Solomon say to keep the king's command? (Eccl. 8:2)

3. Despite the fact that life seems to go well for the wicked, why will it not stay that way? What will happen to those who fear God? (Eccl. 8:10-13)

4. What does Ecclesiastes teach us about our understanding of God?

5. What evil happens to all? (Eccl. 9:1-3) Why does Solomon call it "evil"?

Week 7

Week 7 Challenge (Note: You can find this listed in our Monday blog post):

Prayer focus for this week: Spend time turning your fears into prayers.

Praying	Praise
Monday	
Tuesday	
Wednesday	
Thursday	
Friday	

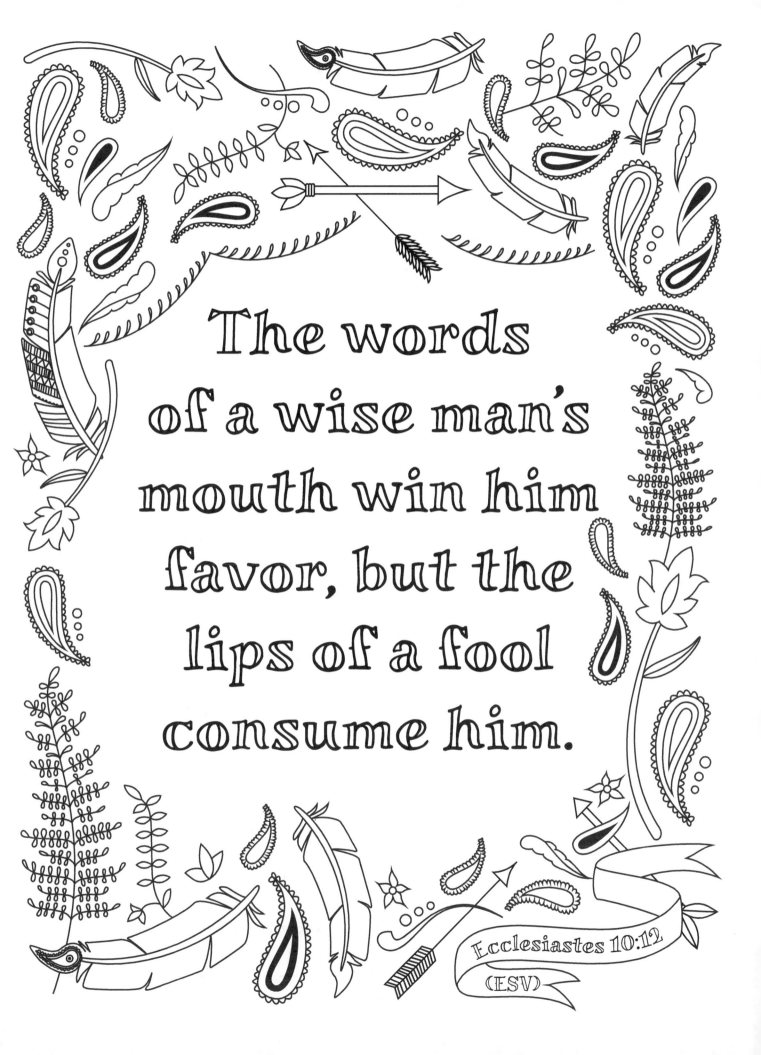

The words of a wise man's mouth win him favor, but the lips of a fool consume him.

Ecclesiastes 10:12 (ESV)

Scripture for Week 7

MONDAY *ECCLESIASTES 9:7-10*

[7] Go, eat your bread with joy, and drink your wine with a merry heart, for God has already approved what you do.

[8] Let your garments be always white. Let not oil be lacking on your head.

[9] Enjoy life with the wife whom you love, all the days of your vain life that he has given you under the sun, because that is your portion in life and in your toil at which you toil under the sun. [10] Whatever your hand finds to do, do it with your might, for there is no work or thought or knowledge or wisdom in Sheol, to which you are going.

TUESDAY *ECCLESIASTES 9:11-18 (ESV)*

[11] Again I saw that under the sun the race is not to the swift, nor the battle to the strong, nor bread to the wise, nor riches to the intelligent, nor favor to those with knowledge, but time and chance happen to them all. [12] For man does not know his time. Like fish that are taken in an evil net, and like birds that are caught in a snare, so the children of man are snared at an evil time, when it suddenly falls upon them.

[13] I have also seen this example of wisdom under the sun, and it seemed great to me. [14] There was a little city with few men in it, and a great king came against it and besieged it, building great siegeworks against it. [15] But there was found in it a poor, wise man, and he by his wisdom delivered the city. Yet no one remembered that poor man. [16] But I say that wisdom is better than might, though the poor man's wisdom is despised and his words are not heard.

[17] The words of the wise heard in quiet are better than the shouting of a ruler among fools.

[18] Wisdom is better than weapons of war, but one sinner destroys much good.

WEDNESDAY *ECCLESIASTES 10:1-7 (ESV)*

[1] Dead flies make the perfumer's ointment give off a stench;
  so a little folly outweighs wisdom and honor.

[2] A wise man's heart inclines him to the right,
  but a fool's heart to the left.

[3] Even when the fool walks on the road, he lacks sense,
  and he says to everyone that he is a fool.

[4] If the anger of the ruler rises against you, do not leave your place,
  for calmness will lay great offenses to rest.

[5] There is an evil that I have seen under the sun, as it were an error proceeding from the ruler:

---

6 folly is set in many high places, and the rich sit in a low place. 7 I have seen slaves on horses, and princes walking on the ground like slaves.

THURSDAY

8 He who digs a pit will fall into it,
  and a serpent will bite him who breaks through a wall.
9 He who quarries stones is hurt by them,
  and he who splits logs is endangered by them.
10 If the iron is blunt, and one does not sharpen the edge,
  he must use more strength,
  but wisdom helps one to succeed.
11 If the serpent bites before it is charmed,
  there is no advantage to the charmer.
12 The words of a wise man's mouth win him favor,
  but the lips of a fool consume him.
13 The beginning of the words of his mouth is foolishness,
  and the end of his talk is evil madness.
14 A fool multiplies words,
  though no man knows what is to be,
  and who can tell him what will be after him?
15 The toil of a fool wearies him,
  for he does not know the way to the city.

FRIDAY

16 Woe to you, O land, when your king is a child,
  and your princes feast in the morning!
17 Happy are you, O land, when your king is the son of the nobility,
  and your princes feast at the proper time,
  for strength, and not for drunkenness!
18 Through sloth the roof sinks in,
  and through indolence the house leaks.
19 Bread is made for laughter,
  and wine gladdens life,
  and money answers everything.
20 Even in your thoughts, do not curse the king,
  nor in your bedroom curse the rich,
for a bird of the air will carry your voice,
  or some winged creature tell the matter.

Read: Ecclesiastes 9:7-10
Soap: Ecclesiastes 9:10

Scripture - Write out the **Scripture** passage for the day.

Observations - Write down 1 or 2 **observations** from the passage.

Monday

Applications - Write down 1 or 2 **applications** from the passage.

Pray - Write out a **prayer** over what you learned from today's passage.

Tuesday

Read: Ecclesiastes 9:11-18
Soap: Ecclesiastes 9:17-18

Scripture - Write out the **Scripture** passage for the day.

Observations - Write down 1 or 2 **observations** from the passage.

Applications - Write down 1 or 2 **applications** from the passage.

Pray - Write out a **prayer** over what you learned from today's passage.

Read: Ecclesiastes 10:1-7
Soap: Ecclesiastes 10:1-2

Scripture - Write out the **Scripture** passage for the day.

Observations - Write down 1 or 2 **observations** from the passage.

Wednesday

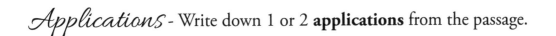

Applications - Write down 1 or 2 **applications** from the passage.

Pray - Write out a **prayer** over what you learned from today's passage.

Read: Ecclesiastes 10:8-15
Soap: Ecclesiastes 10:12-13

Scripture - Write out the **Scripture** passage for the day.

Observations - Write down 1 or 2 **observations** from the passage.

Applications - Write down 1 or 2 **applications** from the passage.

Pray - Write out a **prayer** over what you learned from today's passage.

Friday

Read: Ecclesiastes 10:16-20
Soap: Ecclesiastes 10:18

Scripture - Write out the **Scripture** passage for the day.

Observations - Write down 1 or 2 **observations** from the passage.

Friday

Applications - Write down 1 or 2 **applications** from the passage.

Pray - Write out a **prayer** over what you learned from today's passage.

Reflection Questions

1. Once again Solomon talks about work. What advice does he gives in Eccl. 9:9-10?

2. According to Eccl. 9:13-18, how is wisdom better than might?

3. In what way does folly "outweigh wisdom"? (Eccl. 10:1)

4. What danger is he warning about in Eccl. 10:8-9?

5. What truth do we learn about laziness in Eccl. 10:18?

My Response

Week 8 Challenge (Note: You can find this listed in our Monday blog post):

Prayer focus for this week: Spend time thanking God for how he is working in your life.

Monday

Tuesday

Wednesday

Thursday

Friday

The end of
the matter;
all has been
heard. Fear God
and keep his
commandments,
for this is the
whole duty
of man.

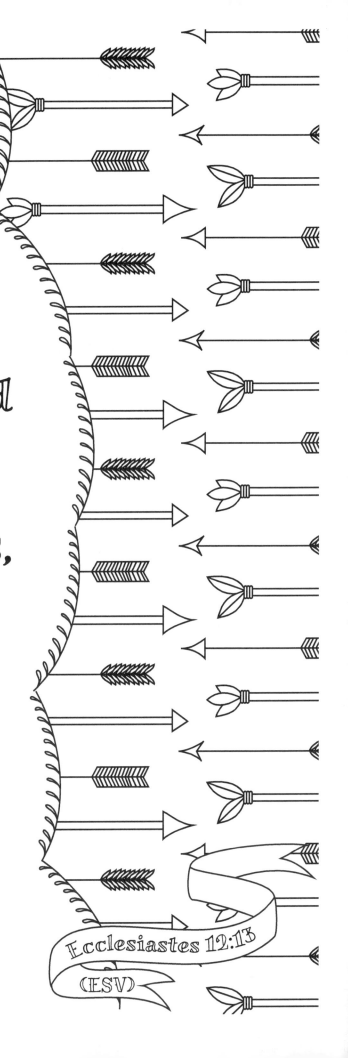

Ecclesiastes 12:13
(ESV)

Scripture for Week 8

MONDAY   *ECCLESIASTES 11:1-4 (ESV)*

¹ Cast your bread upon the waters,

   for you will find it after many days.

² Give a portion to seven, or even to eight,

   for you know not what disaster may happen on earth.

³ If the clouds are full of rain,

   they empty themselves on the earth,

and if a tree falls to the south or to the north,

   in the place where the tree falls, there it will lie.

⁴ He who observes the wind will not sow,

   and he who regards the clouds will not reap.

TUESDAY   *ECCLESIASTES 11:5-10 (ESV)*

⁵ As you do not know the way the spirit comes to the bones in the womb of a woman with child, so you do not know the work of God who makes everything.

⁶ In the morning sow your seed, and at evening withhold not your hand, for you do not know which will prosper, this or that, or whether both alike will be good.

⁷ Light is sweet, and it is pleasant for the eyes to see the sun.

⁸ So if a person lives many years, let him rejoice in them all; but let him remember that the days of darkness will be many. All that comes is vanity.

⁹ Rejoice, O young man, in your youth, and let your heart cheer you in the days of your youth. Walk in the ways of your heart and the sight of your eyes. But know that for all these things God will bring you into judgment.

¹⁰ Remove vexation from your heart, and put away pain from your body, for youth and the dawn of life are vanity.

WEDNESDAY   *ECCLESIASTES 12:1-8 (ESV)*

¹ Remember also your Creator in the days of your youth, before the evil days come and the years draw near of which you will say, "I have no pleasure in them"; ² before the sun and the light and the moon and the stars are darkened and the clouds return after the rain, ³ in the day when the keepers of the house tremble, and the strong men are bent, and the grinders cease because they are few, and those who look through the windows are dimmed, ⁴ and the doors on the street are shut—when the sound of the grinding is low, and one rises up at the sound of a bird, and all the daughters of song are brought low— ⁵ they are afraid also of what is high, and terrors are in the way; the almond tree blossoms, the grasshopper drags itself along, and desire fails, because man is going to his eternal home, and the mourners go about the streets— ⁶ before the silver cord is snapped, or the golden bowl is broken, or the pitcher is shattered at the fountain, or the wheel broken at the cistern, ⁷ and the dust returns to the earth as it was, and the spirit returns to God who gave it. ⁸ Vanity of vanities, says the Preacher; all is vanity.

THURSDAY   *ECCLESIASTES 12:9-12 (ESV)*

⁹ Besides being wise, the Preacher also taught the people knowledge, weighing and studying and arranging many proverbs with great care. ¹⁰ The Preacher sought to find words of delight, and uprightly he wrote words of truth.

¹¹ The words of the wise are like goads, and like nails firmly fixed are the collected sayings; they are given by one Shepherd. ¹² My son, beware of anything beyond these. Of making many books there is no end, and much study is a weariness of the flesh.

FRIDAY   *ECCLESIASTES 12:13-14 (ESV)*

¹³ The end of the matter; all has been heard. Fear God and keep his commandments, for this is the whole duty of man. ¹⁴ For God will bring every deed into judgment, with every secret thing, whether good or evil.

Read: Ecclesiastes 11:1-4
Soap: Ecclesiastes 11:4

Scripture - Write out the **Scripture** passage for the day.

Observations - Write down 1 or 2 **observations** from the passage.

Monday

Applications - Write down 1 or 2 **applications** from the passage.

Pray - Write out a **prayer** over what you learned from today's passage.

Tuesday

Read: Ecclesiastes 11:5-10
Soap: Ecclesiastes 11:8

Scripture - Write out the **Scripture** passage for the day.

Observations - Write down 1 or 2 **observations** from the passage.

Tuesday

Applications - Write down 1 or 2 **applications** from the passage.

Pray - Write out a **prayer** over what you learned from today's passage.

Read: Ecclesiastes 12:1-8
Soap: Ecclesiastes 12:1-2

Scripture - Write out the **Scripture** passage for the day.

Observations - Write down 1 or 2 **observations** from the passage.

Wednesday

Applications - Write down 1 or 2 **applications** from the passage.

Pray - Write out a **prayer** over what you learned from today's passage.

-Visit our website today for the corresponding blog post!-

Thursday

Read: Ecclesiastes 12:9-12
Soap: Ecclesiastes 12:11

Scripture - Write out the **Scripture** passage for the day.

Observations - Write down 1 or 2 **observations** from the passage.

Thursday

Applications - Write down 1 or 2 **applications** from the passage.

Pray - Write out a **prayer** over what you learned from today's passage.

LoveGodGreatly.com

WEEK 8 135

Friday

Read: Ecclesiastes 12:13-14
Soap: Ecclesiastes 12:13-14

Scripture - Write out the **Scripture** passage for the day.

Observations - Write down 1 or 2 **observations** from the passage.

Friday

Applications - Write down 1 or 2 **applications** from the passage.

Pray - Write out a **prayer** over what you learned from today's passage.

-Visit our website today for the corresponding blog post!-

Reflection Questions

1. Life is unpredictable according to Eccl. chapter 11, so how are we to live?

2. Why does Solomon emphasize the fact that we must remember God in our youth? (Eccl. 12:1)

3. Taking the whole book into consideration, why does Solomon say that life is meaningless?

4. What makes life meaningful?

5. What should be our priority?

My Response

Made in United States
Troutdale, OR
04/18/2024

19268917R00080